FLESH
PHOENIX

MITCH GREEN

Copyright © Rad Press Publishing
Flesh Phoenix

All rights reserved. No part of this publication may be reproduced, distributed or conveyed, without the permission of the publisher.

First printing: 2016

ISBN 9780692708590

Artwork: Public Domain:
Bouquet of Flowers in a Vase 1618 Ambrosius Bosschaert

Cover design/Interior design by Mitch Green

She's a flesh phoenix. A stratospheric bombshell.

ONE

Plant Our Bones

This is sacrilegiously staged. Slathered and slandered in segments – inverted, extorted discretely, secreting symptomizing points of interest. We are retorting resplendence as if it came upon us to repent our self-made sins. Picturing places we've been – gone or going, in this intersecting detail of debauched deliverance. We wait for our weight to make the first move. The interlude, the opening act. The prologue where decaying dispositions position the lucky ones the privilege to scarf in tranquility. Take a breath. Shuttle the shy. Harvest the sky, for we coincide collectively off of partnering highs. Mindless. Mildewed. We've been here hope building and faith funding, while the while and everlasting skips town to profit off of other planets – near and a lot less mild, than this wild wide world we plant our bones in.

Floating Facedown

I'm a floatation in a fluid sky, spreading my muscled halo around the rim of the universe, upon, as beauty beats on, I will capture prisms behind these eyes to stream projections of spectral explosions splashing shades to color the faithless atmosphere.

Wet Salt

Your cold, wet warmth, sliding down the arch of my hips. A rolling intolerable sensation shaking to bend a quivering satisfaction to dampen the spoils of my inner thighs. There's nothing quite like the way you move your lips to tongue a feeling into my bones. Cautiously around you work your body, an engine of arousal to stem and stir the throes of your demands. Like wet dogs, we shake the salt from skin, and connect our weight, interrogating the intimacy with a submissive coil. Recoiling conscious foreplay to evolve into a curling of toes and knuckles. White knuckled, knees buckling. Clutch wars. In between the divide of your faith, I find a salvation.

There Are Monsters In Heaven

We ran out, away from all the things that would cause us harm. We left the lights in our old homes on, but filched the décor. Countless, we counted the streets, and all the bed sheets we burned. Our lives, they are changing, and we're leaving, behind the low times, for a wild fire. In a wild life, my darling, tonight, let's burn.

Angelic Alienation

We flicker in on an upside-down spell spaced room. Decorations enveloping - revolving normality. Neatly noxious, teasingly tasteless - facing from ceiling to an unmade mattress, exists also an unlaced, leisurely lying lady. Sultry wear. Bastardizing beauty in diluted dictation of some racy simulation of cute and damaged. Battle black bruises, swollen skeletal contusions - perforations, aftermath of a bomb blasted illusion. Made of realism for play. Praising her buoyancy; made to sway upward into our cosmic correlation. She spaces her fingers in fabrications, signaling the enraged and estranged prodigies from the strange faith of falling face down. Rising. Climaxing. Counting in reverse. Possessed princess in nothing but her waxen world. Closer to our lips. To our reality. To our mental. To the severity of our principle. Possible to taste, to touch, to fuck - she orbits our abortion of existential innocence. Invasive, intrusive, elusive interference of vanity in physical sobriety. She unwinds her tongue to charm, to harm, to alarm, to invigorate us. Her sexuality shadows our partnership. We are the procreative prequel for preview.
She's the perversion of perfection, but perfectly persuading perversion.

Savior

Remember that night?
When In the heights of midnight – out of
touch with ourselves, we touched each
other. We are the audience, the distinctive
identity of various and vast voices
whistling through the cracked windows.
We know nothing but on how to make
waves in this mechanical jungle. Seats
become handbrakes, Head space stolen off
of infusion. Torn muscles, bloodshot eyes,
descending teeth, hands like silver razors
reacting out of impulse. The sounds are
ungodly, like some grating war between
chalk and glass. Our backseat windshield
reflects gravitating sweat. Shuffling.
Rolling. Rambling. Bending. Breaking.
Twisting. Spinning. Exchanging.
Romanticizing the idea of how we are all
simply spiritual. Nothing normal ever
comes out this far – this deep away from
a world where belonging is seen as
something you can call your own.
We are all alone.
Living, loving, fighting, and
feeling in ways that explore
the behavior of our self-serving savior.

Dance Devil, Dance

Flicker in on the face of a car hood. Fierce fog lights
spitting smoke to swivel and scale the spine of a
feminine fragility. Fractured at each jointed
connection. Dancing diva, demonstrative doer of
dares. She's the kind of apparition who causes cars
to crash. Palms against wiper-bladed glass. Knees
knocking notches into our hood. Heavy hitter of
front seat spectators, we, the wheelmen of
retrospective, spare attention to this wiry, spirited
spectacle. Four legged seater, sweet scented
cheater. She shares with us her burning burdens.
Her various personal virginities.
Her stage act.
Her culture.
Her primitive provisions.
Cash crimped to sizzle deep beneath teeth that grip.
Wet woman of transgressional aggression.
Lock the doors from the outside, she says.
Lock us up tight in our suits and tied wrists.
Buckled to the leather.
We're going nowhere. Fiendish fetish.
Soon we'll be one of the same.
There's a blackout in her grimace.
A smile so vile it could filch the enamel to escape our gums.
We were warned. We were given a shot. Two mixed
drinks down. Devil hot. Hell handed us a savior, and
we forgot how she was forged of fevers. Sweating,
we couldn't cool. Contemporarily contrite, oxygen
divorced us. Inhalation of red gloss fumes
concocted in perfume. So strong, even throughout
the emblazoned gasoline waves; our senses caved.

Inertia

The night grew deeper as around me she
moved, smoking grey, warped in absolution,
hinged over and glued together in motion.
She's open, but a burning ocean, and I'm
swimming in circles, learning what kind of
a god could invent such inertia.

Limber Listener

Levitating on a dome, a scalped circle of parted hair presents itself at our waist. Our perception is perpendicular to how this figure is merged comfortably. Naturally nipped and cropped to fit the mix of our mass. Knuckled imposters invade, score the white flesh of her microwaveable cranium. She is the damsel of delicacy. Articulation of abnormality. Different, but differently delicate. She's wispy. A fiber. Limber limbed listener, with an ear soaking up the secreting secrets of what makes us whole. She's melting liquid. A vapor in a whiteout. A pale perversion of what makes perfect, perfect.

Glass Gods

We've seen the day sink to night. Leaves shift shades of autumn burn. Swell and deflate to fall. A cosmic saloon of furnace springs melting into a miasma. Fading in. The trees. The gardens sprite in decay. Glass Gods gleaming through gloss windows. We are not of this place. Perceptions of presences only to furnish; fornicate the formulations of a sealed spherical stage. Human homes owning invertebrate invaders. Last on earth. In a cubic contortion of contouring calibrations. Like a luminous lustrous leviathan leering through plaster pixilation, we were born this way.

Lost and strange.

Bite Open The Scar

Discovered out of bounds, and blending slightly shattered, you were caught touching the sides of us that were lethally loud. Surface surfer, cautiously closed off to others like me, but I suppose you swore on it all that it was always meant to be this intricate. This wild. This free. This overwhelming. This long living. This tamed. This damaged. This pristine. Caught in a solar ecliptic crisis, spaced from scalp to sole, separated cycle of seen scenes. Your layers led me deeper, on depth depletion, and darker days. Bite open the scar, strike the flare, emboss the calm, and quench the storm.

Fire. Fire.
Fire away.

At least in flames, we'll remain warm.

I've never been jealous of lines, shapes and the hue of the untouchable, until the night she came across in nothing but the shadows she wore out of habit.

Imprint

We're drifting sideways through an open space. Serenely spiraling, spinning, spooling - mind swimming in a solution. Our whereabouts aren't on location. Simplistically enough, we're the solidity of an ether enamored to invert. We're collapsing, closing the shade. Meddling to mingle a mold. Washed over in a toxic cold, flooding flush our figure. Dance we do in the dark, blindfolded buffoons beveled black by fragments. Abstractions of artificial affliction. We take note. We modify to bone. We are reborn. We are no longer the placenta of rejection. We are the physical parabola of width and height. Godlike muses thawed and bent out of proportion to placidity. All made to be made - swishing sounds splashing, and we emerge. Our facial imprint sponges back at us through the mirror of heat. After all, we are all atrocious embodiments masked behind meat.

Lover

Swear to tell me you believed we'd come this far away from nothing and everything, only to end up in a place where it is safe to slip out of our skeletons.

And I will swear on our skin that this here, is where we will stay.

Nuclear Nudity

A breath away from hearing a heartbeat over a
sleeping shape - we are invasively close. It hums,
mumbles, and snores as it sleeps. We see it all.
Hear it all. No filter, and no shame. This is art. This
is the world in skin. This is life. What are we doing?
What are our intentions? How come the window to
our left is open? Invasion of entry. Lost morale to
obsessional property. These walls do not own our
home. These walls are delicate. Fragile. Fixed from
the bedroom door to the bedframe. Fiction hasn't
the gumption to be this bold. This audacious. This
over the top. "Do it now" hammers the set of lips
behind my ears. Inside my head, where the
customary mind neglects sleep.
The shape *settles*.
Turns from side to spine.
Move *close*.
The shape *shakes*.
It has a sex.
Nudity.
Soft shaven and simple, yet complex.
She is nuclear.
She is alive.
She is the scar left after a burn.
She is dreaming of all the love she lives.
She is dangerously human. She is,
and I am not.

A Kiss From Bedlam

Patiently, playfully, stationary, and carefully we collapsed in a moment of colossal mishaps, misshapes, and misplacements. Wrinkling, slinking into thwarts of prose, poetics and unconscious love making.

Swim

She was the kind you could swim in if only you
knew how to hold your breath just right.
*But I was more a lover than a swimmer, therefore I
decided to stay forever.*

Soft to Hard

Come crawl me out of this bed, investigate the soft
to hard bits that flare a romantic conflagration.
Instantly combust and let flow the elements
of your design.
A delicate, demanding disposition
shuddering my entire physical.
Cut my core gently in crosses
to brand me yours.

Snubbed

The intuitive, injected illusion insisted on firing away. Out about three miles deep, wide, a wondering wilderness recites how to inhabit a kingdom of interstellar phenomenal proportions. Perspiring platitudes picking poisonous prey for procreation. A streaming starlit lagoon, leeching loud lovers who go on about eating one another, just until the dawn dances on diamond dirt, and ditches serendipity for sadism. Cold play culprit, kingpin of collapse. Sheltered dominance, violent venders defending the disturbed. Creepy crawling killers, shooed away in mass. Shoveled beneath a bulking billow of dead willows rolled in roots and grass, so that one and not two could rest lazily in long lapses, without the need for anything unearthly to surface.
Dead in deathly routines,
we're walking isles of the obscene.
Clinging casually
to warm beds in hopes to extract the imperceptible filth we had aborted, go on, away, where the soil stings the cuts we made.

Epitaph

You are the irrevocable gem of ongoing security.
Every motion that is mutual to beauty.
I see a world in you.
I see stars, celestial simulations diverged
amongst eons on fire.
Skies sloping to skid epitaphs
worth of iridescent stratospheres, scattered
chaotically in every hallucinogenic hue.
Valuing your disbanded illustrative,
I had to take a step back to
absorb in the breathing ritual of ratification.
Because in all this time, I hadn't known that oxygen
had a kill switch until I became coalesced with you.

Hurry Home, Heart

My vessel of fortitude, chapel of completion, my
spherical craft of idealistic, perpetual purification.
An exhale in growth of self, you, the friction and
static, enflaming tantric ways to nurture my nature.
You name me in roads, traveler, traversing over
treaded points of attraction, the windowed walls of
my eyes. A distorted, directional, distinction,
sighting out into the glass shaped shell you hold so
well. Splice us into double sided reflections to
forever face another, long ways, allotting out the
finite for the infinite, by the same manner you flesh

yourself.
Myself.
Ourselves.

Equilibrium

I tangle beneath myself in the roots of her
equilibrium. Transcendence to passage. Safely,
softly, solemnity. I think of God when I think of her.
Inward staring out, all those inexplicable solutions
flushing me away. All the brand new days, shores,
bedsheets, trees, stars, suns, moons, magnificent
myths, scars, the intake of O, the exhale of
neurotoxins, and those sleeves she rolls her hearts with.

Muse

Filtered figure of fervor, feverishly fragile, my darling intensive, vitally ferocious - faith skim to hover, hang above this floor. Oversee this stasis shell, shattered, shaking, we've been sinking, slathered in comas. An illusory, self - evolutionary, invested invitation. We let the rope slip, as did we into suspension. She's love's lyrical resurrection.

Ghosting

Lightly living in love,
I discovered a god with the
same eyes and thighs as her's.
And death, in all that
dead darkness, all really
seemed alive at first.
But now I'm ghosting about -
happily ever haunted
by her sound.

Cube Circus

We are witness to the cubed room loud in volume. The white noise of existing nature has now expired, retired to the audible entombment of a nexus. A circus it is in here. Pronunciations power-rolling together to create babble. Shelling off the exterior level of skin. What lies underneath is hard to believe. A scale-less, in-hideous signification. To stay fighting together, keeping the fibers pressed deep into the mortal leather - she unfolds out to spare the boiling gold, thinning through her casing. Chords pull through chorus lines of auditory pitch. Complacent seductions beneath every niche.

Utopia

Centuries, divinities, infinites, and perforated dimensional hypocrisies fictionalize spiritual effigies to procreate paradoxical utopias.

Cutie

The haze elevates to stoke the ceiling, dispersing to wane from the whips of a zooming fan. It is in the way you see intercourse. It's messy, undignified, unjustly, unruly - a fierce commencement of inaccuracy between two. Shoving, thrusting, pushing through, in the way animals like us behave. Thirsty, the male protagonist pins his lady lover down. Lively alive, he, with a sandpaper appendage pickled in buds, swabs her perspiring plush husk. She is invigorated and appalled all the same. According to the visualization mocking up a must see, must feel event of carnality. The act ceases to perform.
The weight of the room shifts from two, to one rolled on her side, drafting a cigarette from beneath her pillow, up to her lips. Lights the head, and inhales deeply, as if this was her last chemical intake. The man is one of few words. It would appear that he suffocates his feelings, his expressional vulnerability snuggled underneath the weight of his tongue. He just sits, thieving a hit from her oral fixation. Huffs, and finishes off the stick of fire. Up, he lifts from the damp, dented mattress. Littered in chaos. She among the mashup, sits, Indian styled, rolling another smoke. Her shambolic, nakedly nostalgically noxious appearance blends naturally into the scene. Glass walls reflect the hulking profile creeping from view. Alone she sits, left to spit pieces of tobacco off her tongue. Cutie in cold skin, chillingly calm. Anesthetically attached to nothing than the rolling of her thumbs pinching each end of the bud together. Tears teasingly swell behind the padded lids of her irises.

Nose to top lip popping to intensify the sequence of melancholy. The tonic of her blackened cheeks soak the bedsheets. She sniffles. Restores composure, flips the bud in reverse and brands herself. Pressing it. Digging it.
Smudging it in deep against her neck.
Clamped jaws.
Fingers become black from the smoke.
A whimper and then laughter.
Bilingually tasteful in a talent of voicing verbs in words outside of normal mediocrity.

Lastly, beneath her pillow, beside the Marlboro box, is the handle of a loaded gun.
She mothers it
maternally, and strokes it lightly.
Cuticles scratch it softly, constricting to wrap the trigger. Barrel to bedside burlesque.
She directs the directional exorcism at his spine.

Fires.

The room splashes from orange to pink.
Reverberations redecorate the walls in red.
Shellshock kindles our ears to scream, as
smoke and steam mix to screen the scene.

Fossils

Tenderly torqued to warm as I woke. I experienced waves of oxygen wading wide from walls of smoke. Vaporized to stoke a choke, we danced, like two exposed, out of clothed, sensually eloped lovers, leveled over to highly hover, until our fossilized fixations fizzled under.

She's More Than An Entity

Good mornings at noon artistically invite a
silhouette starved skeleton inside my bed.

Living, she lies, drafting hemispheres down under
lungs to control volume of how her spontaneous
layers enliven me.

How hauntingly possessive all of that
flesh to charcoal depiction, complexion to dictation
digests from her mouth in parabolic hexagrams.

She's an image imagined with infatuation, a
contagion in unison of all I've been made out to be.

Sincerely, I'm obviously intoxicated, invigorated,
manipulated on her theoretical, and anatomical
majesty.

Darling

You're a ghost though,
and although I've grown
to go out of my way to
become whole, I slip to forget
the steps you made across
my back yard to the
window I left open,

but I'll let you know how
you taste when you haunt
me the way you do.
In all you do.
Oh, and how you wooed
forth the moves out of
my exoskeletal groove.
Through, it shows and
shines straight, I will hypnotize
you, my filtered darling of placidity.

Because, you're my rouse, my
gist, my powerful, flexible shelling
of what it is that the universe
entitles to be a gift.

Identity

Fluidity flushed our faces
to match the emblazoned
matches ripped to
abandon normality.
We sit.
We stare in conflagration,
on how we are but blinking
distortions behind the tongue
of delusional defilement.
Vaguely bold in pose, she had
crowned queen her reverie,
and I, the fallacy of ethereal
sonnets she slit out through
circumcised identity.
I traversed the travesties of her
buttery flesh, tooth and combed
my way
down,
resounded
and riveted,
torching lightly
to do the
things I
wished
I could do
to her fragile
increment of
inquired invasion.

Displayable, she's the
playable epiphany.
Creases in phased
chins, she chases chills
to chafe religion.

The City Sleeps In Her Head

I had the windows rolled opposite of up to allow the estrogen expression to pardon. Pleasingly petite, she, peacefully, very carefully in casual comfortability previewed that of a perfect passenger.

One whom I could take home.
You know, drift gone with.

She's a lover who creases over every selected segment of leeching longevity, and when she breathlessly breathes out of dimension is when I remember to watch how the painted world of metabolic color frays into shapeshifting surrealism.

Continum

She ricochets illumination past the rift of an equinox.
Adopting carnalities, spiritualties, and a physicality
known to cut out palpable continuum.

Out of who or what we think we need to be, there are realities where what we really are feels more feigned than all the imaginations we believe.

TWO

Volumes

She stood still in broken
fragments of bleeding glass,
Washed into palms of
home-grown flesh;
psychopathic, necromantic,
romantic - lost in mass.
Meddling meaning,
mingles with mad hands;
clapping in rhythmic, rhyming pace.
In dreamscapes you thrive.
Real. Mold - casted to hold.
So close to tongue out the taste,
but what of poison.
Sway softly amid the edge
of pragmatic waste, pouring down.
Where conclusive conscious
strays silent, separated from space.

Vermin

Silent seclusive – reclusive vermin.
Radioactive spiders singing sermons.
Caught in the way your eyes caved –
we saved ourselves. Fought for
replication, duplication of all I had left.
Bended bins – boxing in.
Eating the sulfite solution to
 trigger allergic ends.
Friends swallowed whole –
shallow pasts forgotten.
Again, we are the ones writing riots –
detain our self-righteous.

Dig up the ocean
Resuscitate wonder
Justify this fire - it burns no longer.

Each world we've passed under
Hasn't the charm of the one we
squandered – only invisible ghosts
Boasting of better tomorrows.
Phone the paramedic – too little, too late.
Wait and wake to my call.
Your beauty has always been my
reason, my fall. Learning to live again
seems easier than it sounds.
There are fears at stake – faith to be found.

Set persistence
Molotov the crown.

Dogma

Grace found face in
volumetric mandrakes
 vacating, creating -
making memories.
Deep seeded mistakes
serving infinity.
Divinity, hand off
the trigger - self-pity.
Entities - domesticated
in fire bed cities.
Privative images -
primitive minds, we're
all too involved in
our deadbeat grind.
Tries repeated, defeated
by fictitious signs.
Times like these I wish
you were my hindsight -
reminiscent cry, inventing
rhymes. A fire-eater,
soul-seek and destroy dogma.
Getting our kicks on
the gum-spit drama.
Hit to bash our inner
outcast - vain karma.
Wrong a right, proclaim
and fight the cult coma.
Gone home to mass
a cure. Motif a life
worth living for.
Extort - divorce and
ban the noir.
Rejoice your voice.
It makes for a better world.

Ships & Harlots

I scream her name in vain of sweet imperfection,
you call it a revelation I call it Armageddon.
We're broken from breaking, drowning in salt, I gave
you my heart, yet you say it's my fault.
Lost beneath the lies, deception and hate what does
it take to escape this fate? How long have we been
here, how long have we waited? The lines in my skin
have already faded.

So claim the dead.
Pray for tomorrow.
It's hard to breathe in all of her sorrow.

I hear the voices beneath the water, screaming out, where did we falter? Voices beneath the water, thrashing out, drifting farther.

We are lost!

Of ships and harlots.
Her face is a ghost and I am haunted. Please save me now, I'm scared and alone, I haven't the strength to sail back home. Drowning under the weight of her lies, she hadn't the love to say goodbye. These anchors are heavy, they're pulling me down, Inside the depths of sunken crowns. Inhale my cries and harvest the tears. She is the reason for all my fears.
I hear the voices beneath the harbor, screaming out, where did we falter? Voices beneath the harbor, sinking down, breathing water

Ships and harlots!
She's a ghost.
Ships and harlots.
I am haunted.

Verve

Sinners, saints - bone edged
proficient damsels. Rebirthed
reunions relishing fortified
foundations of burial worship.
To sink, we embalm our bones,
hope, it's not our home.
Nostalgic principles of
dreamscapes and saloons,
dividing oceans.
Monsoons, grave lagoons.
Open up - dead man sounds;
eating floorboards,
wall space and barking hounds.
Stagnant silhouettes in
shallow sand - convergence,
contorted round, into backward
faces - lit in dread.
Steadfast to wake, quaking verses.
Viral fallacies proven to
procreate pallid pardons
of the malice in gloss houses,
spouses sewn at the seam of
mortal dreams. Fiends find
the promise in fractured,
spatter washed mirrors.
Crooked, creepy - screaming things.
On all fours - flapping tongues,
legs lurching, wild teeth chirping,
chatters swallowing fleshed earth.
All is lost and the growls are faded,
the royals rein over the dead and spaded.

1825

I sold out to fade in
On golden, swollen -
swallowed years.
Beginning, I'm feeling
as if I belong here.
Underrated, evaluated as
less a man than before.
Wanting more for an
incapacitated mind.
Remembrance of your shine.
Headlights bending your
fine edged creation,
Illuminating the crystal
daggers from livid eyes.
Whys and how comes,
shift into deadened
when's of then.

Again I'm bent.
Out of place, misplaced soul.
Holding all I can to keep
from losing control.
Be the reason, the solution -
intervention, animosity.
Another decade in captivity,
teases triumphant ends in me.

Dogwood

The dogwood barked,
The fire-grazers sparked.
All in all we felt our
hearts pound and break,
break and shake.
Fake the sake of
thudding normal.

Killers in painted
sneers, smears
clothing scarecrows.
All resurrected for trouble.

They wore pig snouts,
all upon six foot tall
beam mounts.
Posts shooting
short of a moon.

Soon it would fall,
just as us all,
beneath a
harvest doom.

Vermillion

Red wolves bleeding white linens.
Coached supermodel Gods' finding religion.
Picturesque idolized vermilion virgins.
Speaking in consonants, bestial urchins.
Ceremonial pigments snorting estrogen tonic.
Laconic linguistic intimacy, wooing hypnotic
heresy. Lascivious claw-cut
wool, carving, starving jealousy.
Milk-faded heels, and ankles.
Wrists burned in mud.
Spaded spirits of nefarious nomads -
consummation flood.
Freckled topography.
Spinal, seductive geography.
Submissive tease, poster posers.
Prehistoric revival soaking up fire on
worm-earth knees; analytical survival.
Mother morale jaws down on
yawning with moaning throats.
Stoking smoke to asphyxiate toxins,
bare ladies wearing goats.
Ominous aristocrats, masked maidens.
Howling and bleeding white linens.
Red wolves fathering dens.
Alpha-relations.

Static Elephant

She was silent at first.
All but her lips mouthing phrases.
Engorged eyes, filling up
like blue crystal balloons.
An infatuated, pencil and
pen scribbled smile.

Simpleton savior.

In every hour I'm failing.
Can one so many be a part
of the ordinary?
Shadows hosting sunspots.
Alter-egotistic, testing the prolific.
Sensitive silences slithering
into deafness. Communion of
vapor should stand for something.
Post-pardons of previous lovers.'
Lipstick bled covers.
We're all growing in dying skin.
Wishing, hoping and praying for
invincibility to be born.
The mind might find a balance
between miracle and menace.
Digested scorn - upchucking
the deep-seeded.
Depleted, repeated, advancing
passes to obsessive genus.
Mainstream manic.
Tantric panic. An organic mental.
Montage vicious, awkward kisses.
Intimate criminal.

Chameleon

This isn't the way to live,
When will the prayers give?
Survive only to be left behind.
We're finding desire to be set afire.
Inhale, choke – these are
my words smothered in smoke.
Mental insecurity, sense of
deaf clarity. Instant severity.
For vanity, we've lost all passage
to our sanity. Only the aftermath
pushing out the grey foam, I wasn't
built to manage alone.
Through thick and thin,
under the rich and amid the weak,
This'll be the moment I welcome
frustration. Liberation of my own
foiling thoughts. Back and forth,
I'll Colour my demons.
Deep purples to vibrant blues,
Either way, I'll be reminded of you.
You're one in a sea of a billion,
shifting tone like a fucking chameleon.
Feeling faithful to the chemistry,
Yet refusing the symmetry.
The silence, violently heard.
Blister the perseverance of an
eventual finality. Agitating the
carnality to bite.
Tooth and nail, I'll keep on swinging.
Dreaming, screaming while these walls break.
Post your good intentions.
Submit the courage,
Let's reinvent the prevention.
Cease the hurting.
Disowning the person I once
was feels like murder.
Cold hands, wet sand,
evolution of a new man.

Mad Meows

While ingesting confessions on borderline biddings. To renew lease on captured Cthulhus' We'll squander the chatter of a dead English master, and snuff volatile bones blown blue.

Cultivating the clockwork owls haunting hollow grounds in need for fire roasting undead squires. Depravity defines the gravity these dead head fans desire. Morbidity musters melancholic muses to craft and cut reputable attire.

Dreams of mad, unfathomable fiends find playground in these skeletal streets. Whilst creep beggars scarf the barf from hoofed boots, digesting mortality.

It's an ode to passage, unto the deepest, darkest valleys of horror. Swept crypts of cryptic courtyard law. For what master craft had saw were illusionary depictions of vile reflections.

Master of mind-warping visions, all but conflicting his conditions.
A meowing menace to forge these towers of ancient finish.
Historical fictions.

Starfish

We're contemporary -
temporarily plain and vain.
Yet, what I see in her could
be misinterpreted, mistaken
as interrupted perfection.
A complicated blessing,
driven wild with affection.

Part art, part shark.
I'm second guessing
the trade mark she
left on my heart.

20th

I spent my
twentieth
on
Twentieth
Street.
Beaten
between
twenty
tepid tiffs,
and bent
beneath
twenty stories
of tension.
No longer
addicted,
although
ashamed
of commitment.
I paid my
spirit with
dues of
attention
and loved
every minute.

Squares

Reciting foreplay from porno verses -
kicking curbs in bloody converses.
Television boxes televising 50's medicine.
Old western depression -
seducing sessions for clinical confessions.
Inside from the wolfing cries of breaking magic.
We're all sinners strung out on bad habits.

Feel Human

A second passed me by, and in that instance there was a miracle. A blessing disguised in skin. She healed my mind with words she said would cure my nervous heart. Unknowingly, she physically manifested salvation. Pulling me from the deepest, darkest pit of self-loathing into light. What she knows is simply external, nothing quite internal. Never would I have known that these walls could be broken down so quick - so secretly. At long last I see myself.

Durden

I've seen starry eyes dyed white.
Drown alive inside wishing hells
and worm wrung skin tempered in fevers.
Flawed to the opinionated perfectionists
who chew on pregnant tongues.
I was out of mind.
Out of sight.
My tight knuckles balled - knotting rope
to enclose on the tips of pressed lips split sick.
I'd begun the explicit sentence with foul play,
and broken noses. Purple deep in between a
swollen collar, and city streets skinned with rubber.
Asphalt consecrated in teeth and pieces of denim.
My image a mess. Beaten, busted, bleeding,
gloriously defeated with victory.

Astral

The thin sheets between
 us hold no secrets.
Projecting illustrations to
map out imaginary streets,
winding open worlds to
unfold miracles at
each milestone.
We're sleeping,
floating, wandering
carelessly through stormy
skies cooking lightning.
Two unconscious
passengers scaling the
moon and sun, to reach
armored heavens.
One blessing at a time, said life.
One lesson, one strike.
We top pyramids,
we mount mountains for levitation.
Picking prayers from the atmospheric
web to be read like letters.
Soul notes to be returned
with interventions.
Swallowing mouthfuls of
ambition, we scream –

Carpe Diem! Carpe Diem!
Carpe Diem!

Gravity

This dirt smells of old fire.
This room, in her voice feels
less dark. Sleeping with the
incubus, I follow the night into dawn,
washing my flesh in rivers,
in volcanos, in hurricanes,
and tsunamis.
I think of rooftops.
Windows,
busy streets.
I think of deadbeats
selling advice.
Of the spinning world.
Of soured sex.
Of life, love and death.
How the mice,
the roaches,
worms, beetles,
blue moons, lampshades,
color televisions,
books, notepads,
this bed,
and
gravity all communicate.
Of
beggars on Broadway Boulevard.
Of town cars hydroplaning
Into cash bars.
Of
legs sweating perfume.
The shadow smoke,
acceptance speeches.
Clapping hands,
and trophy stands.
Through my secrets you browse,
little snippets on preview.
Come inside, come inside.
Inside out
I'll love you.

3rd Wheel

Crooked teeth
cranked spine
swollen fingers
spent mind.

Twisted gut
splintered skin
swallowed grins
sheltered in.

choking up
spitting rust
thinning buff
fucking love.

3rd wheel
just as usual
fuck it all
I'm the usable.

Beautiful This Way Comes

I met her in a café downtown. Exactly when the long hand landed seven. Alone, she'd been sitting with starlit eyes holding dreams, and reflecting back magic.Kismet conversations over microphones, atop rooftops and well into sunrise. She told me how beauty befell the earth and of open minds meant for worth. Kindred spirits - she and I shared dreams and spent pasts of worlds, and vast knowledge. A sweet, unique mix. 6 weeks passing and I'm a heart lift on stereo rifts, temping my jukebox blood to dance with her rhythm. Soundly talented, alive inside the lines of her grin exhaling serendipity. Entranced in moments found for making, I allowed her the key to my keepsake. Something out of a silent movie. With all the colors, popping out the black and grey. Spot lit silhouette casting mirages of her frame.

Still in motion,

I could feel the room spin around commotion.
But she remained, and that moment continues
to circle like a record to the recorded beat of conscious.
The way she kept swiping her glare, mesmerized
I ensnared her stare.
I knew if she too had insight inside
this wild fire of mind, I too could
make her mine. And we connected
on levels, on plains, on pages, in space,
in scenes, in screens.
And when I look at her, I feel peace.

A heart starter.
A starter of heart.
She's a musician of God's grand art.

Animalistic Science

We hid our shadows around lit fires of open nature. With mother earth and all her pleasures inside a silhouette stowaway. I watched the brown planets in her eyes revolve, twist and turn just as heartbeats rotated gravity. And held her waist, bones and face inside that space bed of ultimate duplicity. With harmony and fire mixing, she tames my nervous storm to install a calm. Partaking in counterpart charm, she lies down to bathe mutuality, and the explicit science of our animalistics. Still caught between my fingers, I smell her will, her love, passion, commitment, loyalty. The intimate levels of completion, arousing an awakening to begin. Off the end we dive, tucking and rolling, grabbing and pulling. Our teeth marks leaving behind scars to clothe our untamed hearts. She's an exquisite paramount of longevity. This deep to surface with sensitivity. She's a kill shot eradicating hurt. A vicarious scream weaved within wants. I see I'm where I belong - in this pod built of two naked souls. I held her weight atop, and breathed her in like menthol. It wasn't enough, I couldn't find satisfaction of the flesh she fashioned from the lips of God. I just inhaled, feeling all her wet ends compromise every flaw I had. Wrapped in revelations, I found a new scripture written inside the lines of her thighs. One for resurrection, one for salvation. One for the declaration of subliminal solitude. This earth quaking sunrise tilts until the sleepers sleep, dreamers dream, and lovers love. Our miracle is those of many. Harmonizing chemistry to realign the fervor. A fuck away from igniting the night. A touch away from control. Tonight we'll feed wolves to sheep, and eat the moon whole.

2.0

I dreamt of
avalanches
piling down
in waves of
the noir
narcotic,
in rage
to bleed
the straight
edge. Count
me in, count
me all over,
I'll pull you
in and romance
you under.
Squeeze my
bones make
me a believer,
press your lips
to the loaded
receiver.

We, The Playful

There we were, locked in position. Her legs over mine, fingers tangled. Lips pressed to exterminate distance. She's a tease, a playful romantic lover chewing at the end of my tongue, sucking dry the color. I felt her wetness in my mouth, her nurturing nature to extort sensual nerve. I dried her spit with mine, and thumbed the smooth line of her chin. Her heat pushed me to counterattack. Sending waves and vibrations to swell beneath my core. She hadn't known what she had done, she just sat stroking the length of her hazel hair. Eyes overly hazed, cheeks burnt in blush and those timid lips quivering. If I would've told her, it would have doused the realization of carnality. I fed her my tongue. Her hand brushing against me. Now she knew. She giggled, snickered, let loose that cute and irresistible charm she bestowed inside. I just sat, biting my cheek, trying to contain myself. Restraining from taking her right there in the center of public view. Fuck it, we'd make a fine specimen to examine. But I withheld, combing back the strands of loose hair behind her gentle lobes, and counted every breath she exhaled with an open mouth.

"Do it."

She said it with such demand that I felt shivers. I had managed to control my mechanics. From toes to fingers, breasts to thighs. Crawling a flavor to explore. We couldn't contain it. She had her head pushed back against the seat, her face in direction. God, I wanted it. I wanted her. Her body, her flesh. I wanted to eat her up. All these illusions floored my imagination when we started towards the city. How she'd bend apart, of the sound to reflect from the floors to walls. The sensation of her depth. Fighting the wheel, I entertained the feverish warmth soaking within the crease of her hip. The photographic reels came spinning behind my eyes again. Flipping through like a sketch book - of her heels to roof, in nothing but great lighting. Her expressions weighing to narrow concentrative brows and eyes of sexual hostility. But it was all in mind, except for her handheld choke working me graciously.

A flood flogged the roads, all roads promised with any destination of success, and we were left aimlessly searching, frustration pinning us. She wore it beautifully, and I only dared to dream of quenching it. I kissed her wrist, fingers and lips. I needed more, she needed more, but our time was fading. Foreplay for the century.

This desire is evolving into a craze.
Soon, very soon when the universe
aligns, we'll dance inside one another,
and ignite the fucking hemisphere.

Private Worship

Swollen skies had been replaced with creeping blackness and the atmosphere held vigorous, energetic hormones. Lost from awareness, we had slipped away, vowed out into the seclusive solitude of our own private worship. Whole in our primitive values, we extorted ourselves to find the eccentric necessities we so long craved. One another committed to the practice of each other's secrets. She had many hidden along her curves, to the acoustic recoil of her volumetric requests. All in range of my qualifications. The heat washed the windshield and mirrors, even our slippery silhouettes dancing through a shadow sedation of blissful rocking. Breaking fevers had never pressed out toxins quite like that night, and still I reflect on the sensations of mass strictures reigning away within muscle. Of the shift in climate, of how the tight spaced interior held two vibrantly spastic soul breeders, abolishing time to concentrate on the triggers of pleasure. The aftermath only proposed that we lie awhile to morph into arms, legs, chins, elbows, feet and hearts. Counting every line, freckle, and birth blemish branded into our creative collaboration. She in all her emotions, wore the ether with royalty. A delicate design demanding an encore. Until the sun burnt elastic holes in the oxygen globe, and the trees made appearance, we consistently carried on, matchmaking our bodies to medicate under meditation from behavioral addictions.

Labyrinth

She sat there in a
fever, prolapsing
and sweating fire.
Rapturously rounded
in warmth, shedding
self-born sins into a
vast valley of verbose
epression. Exorcising
 suppressions to sell
my soul with, I,
compelled to her gist,
fed my price on her
roaring soul.
Wired her
bones beneath
bewitched secrets,
foiled in fanatical
resilience, creased
her waxed weight
into 6 different
folds and ate
her whole.

Love Over Night

The silence.
It creeps, crawling
carefully through
these walls, up
winding stairs,
over the balcony,
through the halls,
and into my room.
She, the ghost.
Quietly calming
her shade to wither
wildly around my
 perched breaking.
I can't stand these
four corners.
This palace,
temple of
stagnant enclosure.
It's suicide.
My neurotic
logic contrives
ridiculous fictions
of her being out
late with another,
dancing in his
covers - spilling
my love on
the carpet like
cheap wine.

Kink

I took hanger pins to her nipples, and watched her squirm blindly, biting roughly, violently down on the ball stuffing her teeth. She wet the table, flushing a current to bathe her thighs. Red, polished pink and raw. Constrained, captivity confined her kinks. The way she implemented savage demands, solid and subtle, just how I imagined, just how I liked it. She had no say, no authority or dominance to tease. She could only beg, whine for my touch to penetrate her deepest quirks. Sweet and sour satisfaction streamed from her mouth. Knees vibrating, arms shivering - was she coming from anticipation, or of my throb that slammed inside? Breaking the barriers of sound, the clapping storm of whips and chains - manipulated the atmosphere to jive with her motive moans. Over and over, fucking and slapping. Catching her throat to further pleasure, I for good measure and fairness unleashed my girth to replace the bond in her lips and forced her to swallow. Her legs quaked as I finished her off, feeling her tense. Orgasms manifesting like warfare.

1,2,3,4 - When she rounded 5, she collapsed in ecstasy.

Testosterone

We see knuckles that are pop cherry red soaking the bathroom floor. A man's face flushed in long lost hope, with eyes beaten blue, bruised all the way down through his nose and lips. Busted Reflection, a shattered mirror, and his chest that heaves in sporadic formation. There's a dead man in the corner, next to an old, cracked, blood battered tub.

His face is gone, rid of bone construction and shape. In his hands we see a switchblade free of damage. Back to the man in the mirror, obviously the victor. He spits a cord of metallic with teeth into the sink, straightens his crooked tie and exits the washroom.

Mirage

As I lie here
after 11:00
Flipping ideas
of pages.
Of her,
her body,
hair within
ivory skin,
lips and
tongue.

How she slips
asleep to speak
of love.
I imagine an
outline,
silver casing, and
crafted warm.
Her, floating fire
on
the peak of a
soaring dawn.

Baptism

On my way out,
she decided to go all in.
Wet skin, a spine that
panned down into the
folds of what could
be baptism. Undressed,
she cocked a glare over,
nipping a hole at the
corner of her lip
and slithered into a
wave of carbonation.
Clouds rolling above
outside these walls
couldn't compare to
the white fuzz leaching
her body. Legs bent,
arms rowed in reverse,
a neck to chin, teeth licking,
loving work of perfection
demanding my awe.
She saw, she knew, giggled
and pulled me in with
her and all that skin.

Ink Maid

If I could open myself up
without the visceral mess,
I'd hand out my emotions
all in color. And as you
roll around soaking the
diversity of blues and reds,
pinks and black, golds into
glowing greens, I'll print
photos of you. Swirling,
swimming, and spinning -
I'll make love to you in all
that ink. No one mentioned
the making of art messy, they
didn't have to. She sprawled
out beneath me, slipping wet
like an oiled down mermaid.
Five fingered fins, linguistic
lips fit for a sailor. *"Salty Captain"*
she called me, slurring sarcastically.

Purity

As we fade in on this empty street of darkened cars and dead city lights, We are inflicted by an intense fear of dread. The thin, light rain sprawling down to pool and pelt against gravel sends a vibe of distant menace and sleeping innocence. We hover above the silent vicinity of nothing suspicious and float upwards so to pass through the heights of over lingering trees. Down we dip, through a neighborhood of half-lit homes - a residence fit for a domestic safe haven. Cars are parked in place on driveways, curbsides, among untrimmed lawns. There stand among the porch side a couple of swaying silhouettes and rambling laughter. Conversational status to the resemblance of college disposition. We pass through their banter and zoom through into the front door, across the occupied den of not so civil, appropriate participates - and find way to the stairway. It leads up, up higher around to another set that winds into a selection of doors. The bathroom ahead that lies open in light to expose a half-naked couple smothering one another. The suave shaved son of explicit behavior has this Barbie doll designed babe perched on the sink, her glossy fingers trailing cuts through his hair, as his are weaving up her skirt. This is the house of sin. Home of sexual expedition. The next room is no different, here rolls a band of tangled body parts, ripping the greasy sheets - masked by kneecaps and armpits. Orgiastic at best, and if you're a freak, a play thing, a submissive, dominant dealer - then this here, inside these four walls stocks roost to your vices and niches. This little partition of society doesn't exist in daylight. Dawn dials the neighborhood back into these science projects who pretend to be your doctors, Insurance agents, and white-collar bosses. Even they still hear the naughty, plastic queen whining through the shower wall.

Danger, Danger

From the distance
she moved in an
abstract body of
shimmering gas.
Fluidly shimmying,
flapping her wet bones
to melt into a fog.
And as she splashed,
I noticed the candles
evenly situated
around the rim
of my bed.

This bed,
our bed.

The bed we made
love in. And as
absorbed as I had been,
I knew she was
a bit dangerous.
But I liked danger,
more than I liked myself.

Friction

I watch her sitting. Length of hair idling over the whips of eyes. And in the moment I cannot feel the breeze, nor the heat sticking sweat to skin, but only my chest, expanding to deflate in and out of unison. Oblivious, she carries her smile to me with friction. Then is when I realize that I am the luckiest bastard on this planet, to know the limits she inspires within, to touch her, listen to every word slip through lips and splash away all my insecurities. It's like sifting the salt from the sea, pulling the shine from diamonds. There is no place, no division, soul charming enough to ever make me leave. In the depths of her watering eyes, rivers brimming over, I pull her into me, squeezing together our hearts, and I assure her of this. I've found the one who conquers my demons, settles the score of sorrow, and casts out frivolous fear. She's made waves in my emotions. She's picked up the pieces of my brokenness.

Little danger,
Little lover,
Together,
we'll fight
for one another.

Marvel

Freckled
and
dressed
in
nothing,
she
strings
a
smile
together
with
teeth.
And
in the
way
she
loves
to listen,
I'll
forever
be the
sound
to her
sleep.

Nymph

Screaming, I found her sprawled, spine spanned in the center of the room. Legs expanding at each end, toes curling, and the arch of her neck welcoming me through thin eyes. She had the length of rubber rolling between her fingers, in and out, some warming routine to cast out the morning poison. I felt the shiver of cold sweat swell beneath my buttoned wrists, dampening the fabric to bleed a new shade of white. The publicity stunt held at my preview, had her gushing with premediated mass masturbation. Colorfully airbrushed, this porn star acrobat performed her talents like a trained whale would do in front of the media. The more, the more she moaned. The more she tested out the elastic durability of her limits. Swollen already, from pink to blue silicon, pyramid crafted handiworks. All originally selected by her knack in craftsmanship. She'd switch, altering between woods to rubbers, from glass to plastic, as if this experimenting nymph, took her length and quality meticulously. Shoulders curved at the neck, knees just visible below her two, petite pieces of artificiality, she opened her narrow eyes so wide, wider than I'd ever seen. Bulging bolder, brighter, with a mouth slurring slang not fit for parental tyrants of censorship. She opened my imagination. And I'm not sure if it was the way she appealed to me in naked contrast, or the sounds of her abnormal patterns of breathing, but that night I fell in love with female anatomy.

Sheet Eater

It was one of those nights,
with the dims enchanting
the room to a placid hue,
the bed made so that the
end of the sheets were
rolled and tucked, dividing
a partition between the
rustled, feathered headrests
and a lounging lady, with
her dirty feet sleeping sound.
She had been here before,
needing a getaway to crash.
How could I refuse a little
runaway like her, ebony
curls contacting the cutout
of her healthy hips, bronzing
into the scheme of different
colors. I've always found her
to be somewhat of a kosher vice.

Silver Skin

I'm roaring white
lines into the destination
of a silver something.
My hands are heavy
hooks, hanging loose
into every awkward
invitation I have ever
took. Look alive, look
strong, look confident.
Erase the disgruntled
makeup you've smeared
in like clay. It'll make
horror masks look
comfortable, cozy
and cute in all the
displayable dismay.
On rocks, in rows
of all the lights fighting
to glow, she is the
only brightness.
The only star in a
returning blackout.
A chemical cookbook.
An illusion inside a high.
A composition without
the sketch marks.
All that is good,
without the bye.

THREE

Like Flies To A Fawn

We're captivated instantly by a brooding, brown eyed beauty. She's rugged, desolate, and decrepit. A train-wreck queen of the street. Her lips loud in lavish, lascivious color. Smeared and stroked to smother the pretty absence of a smile. This defeated depicted damsel of diluted dissipation, performs privately to caress exposure. Bold, bald swathed body of bronze grain - gravitating to be textured terrain. Finely, she fondles her elemental self, exercising the expedition of experimental energy - unencumbered to explore her selfish deathless.
Independence tows astray diminished façade of faint dependence. She's visual context - a venue all for imploring enhancement of an oceanic, photogenic sky. Mountainous, her power is monstrously moving apart the natural Neptune of the sexually physical.

The damp detox of grotesque.
The arid amplification of a noise.
A burst in the gender bender of
suitable. She's a special, salivating
spade of special. A grandeur girl
aborted by gracious debauchery.

Delirium

Down a detour of delirium.
Diversifying the solidity of self.
Contouring contrast of
conscious confusion,
we are arbitrarily amble,
available to combust
into a collective component.
A mechanism.
A motorized machine of manmade ingenuity.

We are the lucid,
living liquid that
vilifies virgin veins.

The faint vanity.
The unbecoming virus.

The detached misplacement
of muscle. We are every move
maneuvered manually to
create nothing. We are solarizing
divine intervention. The delirious -
subliminal and sublime cortex
of compassion. The darling of
doubts, dependent division of
dreamy - really ethereal. Sightless,
this world knows nothing of
substance abuse when you
inhabit mine the way you do.

You are more
than the combustion
of stars dusting off
space's abstract
depths.
More than
the sea's
tepid
turmoil
storming
gravity
to collapse
together
into one
electric
symphony.

Fishblood

Our human warmth.
Our Lazarus lines.
Our faceless skeletons.
Our cryptic creations.
Our sectional shadows
shedding holographic
dynamos of death.
Our latitudes and
horizontal heavens.
Our provocative paranoias.
Our savvy sadism.
Our naval metamorphosis.
Our passiveness.
We are various.
We are careless.
We all care less and less.
We are changeless by change.
We all revolve inward instead
of outward. We are our own
organism of organs and atoms.
We are pending permanent.
We are the parted promises
down the scalp of
dogmatic dominance.
We are nimble and nude,
nude and nimbly nauseous.
We are a globe of ghosts
bullying the haunted.

Exorcism

Living lights light up
the darkest spaces of
this lifeless nebulas.
We are the colorless
epitome of absolution.
The cathartic
epiphanies
moseying and
rambling
onward through
perdition.
We are flaccid
and flattened
upon our belly
and bones.
Nothing is known here –
separated from
spirit and spirituality,
sex and sexuality.
We are the sleeping
sleepers designated
to a deathless orbit.
We're the lost,
lone lovers left
out for discovery.

These flexible bald bodies are as slick as water.
Eccentric instruments mimicking the promiscuous.

FLESH PHOENIX

She's auburn
audio, punk
and progressive.
Like a favorite
record, perpetual
and invasive.

This life
has been
the best
it has ever
been since
you came
along.
You are
the foundation
to which
I frame
pyramids on.

The howling
opaque
seas
sailing
my
heart
home.

I digested
a girl who
has always
had a way
with claiming
my ether,
enfolding
the stars,
and inverting
the universe.

Aerials & Anchors

Wild like a dream,
she's kismet and
kinetic. A lucid
existence submersing
aerial anchors to
gravitate god.
Alive, we're living,
aloud, she's loving.
Coaching starry
coasts to carry
away our vessel,
out and above
into the plethora
of supersonic
memory. We
have survived,
endured, nourished
internal infernals
by the weight of
heart. Ever and
onward, surmounting
higher upon
levitation - elevating,
lingering to experience
the surface of her
romantic halo. Of
her homeland heaven
exhaling beautiful
breathing. Of her
sublime ether,
revolving circular
around my globe.

She's my moon.
She's my solace.
She's my spiritual regime.
She's the stars in the ocean.
She's wild, wild like a dream.

I'd like to ensnare the arson
in her bones, *warm the fire*

I only want
to build a
life in the
God design
of her eyes,
and live
everyday in
absolute
vulnerability,
belonging,
growing,
forming a
body, a prism,
a shape, a
kingdom,
a universe.

She has been ciphering universes.
The skinless abstraction, the deadly dreamy.

Diamond Dawn

An emerald body of salt splashes fluidly across shimmering sand. Wild, rooted palms dance, bowing down to mingle with the horizon, while an orange iridescent dawn sets the scenic tempo of two walking silhouettes. IVY and LANDO. Their sway saying more than words ever could - their bodily lingo loud enough to magnetize the ocean tides. We hear the laughter, embrace the invisible scent of mutual chemistry, and we walk with them closely. They row their blended wrists back and forth within the whipping wind of passion. And in the moment, they conform to their own spacious, heart-spoiled world, where words slip from mouth to ear, and with eyes to lips they transcend cohesively - wound around one another like breathing fixations. Baptizing feet at the edge of crawling salt, they entertain a spot soft enough to sit. Lando compliments their roost with a couple of branded bottles - comfortably celebratory.

Her words are faint, empty upon the feedback of gusty air, but their alluring, vibrant eyes ponder with deafening delicacy.

IVY - *"When we are plains apart, and the sun has no way of reaching both of us, will you still wait for me?"*

Lando intimately brings her mold more closely, comforting her question without the need for language.

LANDO - *"You better believe that all of my heart, no matter the distance or weight it might endure, will forever belong to where yours beats. This isn't temporary."*

He brushes away the shine from beneath her eyes, words becoming transformed into movements, visually bold, colliding into each other with similar force as the bowling, bustling current ahead of them. For a while they rest and attend the audible sensory of everything, witnessing the ascension of a golden radiant globe.

IVY - *"I haven't known a single moment since you came into my life, where I felt alone. Even when we are monuments away, your presence remains."*

Humans like Ivy and Lando were made gentle. We see their luxurious life, their living love so profound in measure, it is hard to comprehend - to compete with. An entirety of a day is exhausted in the company of themselves, flicking through memories, soundless through time of past to present. We resonate with this reality of hours and years spent separated. Daylight commences to wane, dissolve below the line of sky and sea, and the sight of this seaside dwelling switch into a location of picket houses and parked machines. This is Lando and Ivy ending their day together, their day of connection and realignment. She looks at him, caringly and devotedly - with all the love a universe could conceive. We perceive its power pledge forth a downpour from the hue of her eyes, and we feel the strength within her peel. They share a farewell romance, before a uniformed Lando departs his heart and home to catch his leave.

Over earth we lay, lying out loud to serpents, and harvesting holy hells for the rampant righteous. We are worth no less than gold. No more than diamonds.

The angle of
her vessel,
heaven bound.
Glittered in
liquid earth.

The Rabid

A blast of brilliant light separates the earth and sky.
Filtered gravel garnishing the glow and grit of glorious
existence. Surreally sensational, a sensual scenario.
Sweetly sexual, as she lies, sleeping before me.

Before me, barely sleeping, bare and afraid,
sacred and scared. Slimming dead in depths
of discographic segmentation. She becomes
the single archetypical animal.
The rabid romantic.
The defective atom
pending perilous
evaporation.

She implodes *spiritually*.
She's exposed *privately*.
She stirs steam and smoke to stream arousal.
She's white hot.

A hot petite picturesque,
falling to pieces at the seams.
Abducting me savagely,
darling, abduct me violently.
Extract the imagery, all that
is me physically. I want to
be rid of woes, of worlds,
of religion, of existing.
I want the planets to collide -
I desire to taste the
finite morph me.

Solar Avenues

These are the avenues of depleted vital,
resolutions reflecting back streams from
solar heavens - hues spawning
dimensional dreamscapes.
Cosmic showers shatter arid fire.

Warm tongues heating homeless hope.
Procreative energies let swim
spinelessly through plasmid prayer.
We hydrate hydra tides, and sift skinny
to skim debris out of space.

We are the aspirational
astronauts who forgot
to seek oxygen on the sun.

She's a liquorish caged hexagram praising seance water.

She's a womb weaver.
An earth creature of
city sand and midnight
shimmer.

www.ingramcontent.com/pod-product-compliance
Lightning Source LLC
Chambersburg PA
CBHW032045290426
44110CB00012B/955